# Insomniatic
[poems]
Valerie Fox

BOOKS

Regional Publishing, National Voice
A division of Philadelphia Stories

Regional Publishing, National Voice
A division of Philadelphia Stories

PS Books
93 Old York Road
Ste. 1-753
Jenkintown, PA 19046
www.psbookspublishing.org

Published by PS Books,
a division of Philadelphia Stories, Inc.
9780990471592

Copyright © 2017 Valerie Fox

No part of this book may be reproduced or transmitted in any forms or by any means, electronic or mechanical, including photocopying or recording, or by any information storage or retrieval system without permission in writing from the publisher.

Cover Image: ©2017 Arlene Ang
Book Design: Andrew Whitehead

# Contents

1 Insomnia
2 On Insomnia (Chapter 1)
3 A Watch in a Dream
5 If You Dream About
6 Her dress shows she has abstained
7 For that matter, what does it mean to be human?
9 In the fire alley a rift opened up
10 My Daughter Listening to Christian Tetzlaff
11 That wakes you
12 Two Important Questions on Ant Individuality
13 I'll come see you
15 Letter to Legal Advice Columnist
17 A Point on a Map
18 Here is my story, magic not included
20 Kinds of dramming
21 Two Important Questions Concerning Seahorses
23 Fairmount Ave.
24 Incorruptible
27 Acknowledgments

*To check in, briefly, on the quality of mind and heart—*
  Melanie Farley

# Insomnia

But lately, we are all afraid
to call upon one another
unless the meeting has been pre-arranged.

Must mean someone's personal
Dark Age is looming across
the countryside,
heading toward the cities,
dragging blood and bone.

What did Dalí paint
when he couldn't sleep?

I must've been drunk or invisible
when I used to know facts,
like that.

# On Insomnia (Chapter 1)

The minor expert has a corner room with three windows. A window before it's a window is a hole. The hole idea holds up splendidly with our nighttime ratty-bathrobe-person, making one last encore bow (time-stamped 3:45).

You ask a whole bunch of sleepy-headed awake people to write down their thoughts. That's how we usually think of insomnia research. But some insomniacs forget to use verbs and pause, glance at their hands. Are these insomniacs really not sleeping? We query like that.

"In" means "no" in some cases, as in the word, "insomniatic." Like in the word "invalidate" which is a real word, and in "invalorize" and other made-up words like "insomniatic." "Insomniate" used to mean put to sleep.

Many houses nowadays instead of having attics have crawl-spaces. There must be a reason. Even for curious children, attics are more fun than crawl-spaces. You can see what might be lurking in the attic, say a snake or a rat. But you can't see the spiders tumbling about in a crawl-space.

It's getting to be more and more of a stretch to ponder
    what life was like
here, in the basin
how fires started, where trees pointed

before humans.

Insomeinstancesinsomniaisjustinyourhead.
Inothersitispiecesrattlingacrossthefloor.

# A Watch in a Dream

Tilting and in pursuit
an action repeated ten times
the hour hand pointing
at words that start with "T"

The number ten is self-important,
self-appointed number ten
means a poor outlook

My ancient enemy sidles up to my coupons
Enter the advertising
industry

I have this negative in my hand
I'm hoping my hand won't get too hot
because that will damage my negative

The vanishing point is the point
you notice first

The leaning line of the tree copies
the line of my tall Grandmother

What's that dog doing there?
She didn't like to clean up after
animals such as a lounging retriever

When I look at her backwards
long enough
it starts to reveal something normal
and deep

I'm like that Dickens character
who prostitutes his daughters, sort of,
*ever the child*

If You Dream About

# Her dress shows she has abstained

Her dress shows she has abstained
from productive employment.
For a pretense she has pockets.
She has ideas.
She won't throw them out.
They exist and not just in her thoughts.
In her house her closet her box, drawer or chest, maybe in there.
It takes her more or less time each season to develop aesthetic nausea.
She reserves days, lines them up, like people she hates.
She has this saxophone idea playing and plying
near the end of her song-life.
She can carry water with bare hands.

## *And for that matter, what does it mean to be human?*

(asks Mark Lowe on his birthday)

This question is more important
than plenty of others.

Usually I am asked questions about which song
I should sing for my audition

or what I would do if I were a seahorse
or what I would ask Mr. Walt Disney if I could.

Being human is different than being a seahorse, I guess.
Mr. Walt Disney had a nice accent, and an optimistic

personality, perhaps, I haven't looked it up
in Wikipedia yet. But if his concrete handiwork

tells any story it's one about
waking up and still being alive.

That is not the same as being a good human
or having a good ear.

People can learn to have a good ear
and sing well.

People might do well to practice their singing.
A song doesn't have to be an old song to sing well.

Once there was this fairy in the forest
named Oberon who played a trick

on some humans. You know this.
We all know this.

Donkey ears are always good to laugh at.
And if only we sang, instead of staying silent

or muttering incoherently, actions might get done
more quickly or with less fuss

about who said what and when.
Well, anyway, what does it mean

to be an animal is a question
I want to throw out there, to all the humans.

# In the fire alley a rift opened up

A rift opened up. No one called for help.

People in line commiserate,
forming their own histories.

Without warning the crowd turns
into an animal, and after that
a new car smell.
Unable to refrain any longer
from speech I make a speech.
Somebody has to.
Basically to repeat what we
overhear.

First, what the young cashier said into her phone:
*This morning I had a life.*
*You still have one. You don't love me*
*anymore.*

Second, of my own invention: about boxcars,
some bad TV watching habits.

For certain days, weeks, months
our argument in print
dies down.
This follows the alley part

a kit, a torso.

# My Daughter Listening to Christian Tetzlaff

My daughter fell asleep listening
to Christian Tetzlaff.
All 9-year-olds should experience such luxury.

I was disappointed that my daughter
mostly slumbered through
his Selections from Signs, Games

and Messages by György Kurtág, miniatures
that encompass a "unique world
of naked nerves," multiple voices, tingly details.

Too tired I guess.
She was mildly attracted to the spaghetti strap
girl in front of her

seated in the balcony-right front row,
her lengthy hair and upper body
leaning into air

toward the emotive virtuoso, like she was his
Juliet and his hands were
signaling capitulation.

Jolted awake, finally, by the crowd's cheers
my daughter faintly registered
Tetzlaff's smiling encores—

his Paganini
his Bach.

# That wakes you

that wakes you u[p]. It's a fox racing down the hill in y[our] neighbor's front yard, then racing across your patio, staying off the road for cars. (No one may be[lieve] you, you didn't take a picture. . But try hypnosis for forgetting.)

**Fever:** Dreams of illness should not send you sprin[t]ing to the doctor. A sneezing car ba[by] points to a natural cleansing proc[ess]. If you follow your tail and turn in circles for many hours you will sta[rt] to understand your place in the w[orld]. *(Try this four or five times.)*

**Filmic:** Esp[e]cially that part where you're trying to rub tar off your hands at 2 a.m. more awake than you thought. Also that time you knew you were talkin[g] to Benjamin Franklin wearing a m[ask]. Also when the eating of white ca[s]seroles became fairly common as an ice-breaker. Also calendar da[y]s that went unmarked, alas. You ha[d] this romantic idea about being able to play chess all the day long with g[y]psy tunes a-playing in the background. You encounter that part of yourself daily on the streets of your town, alive [with] humans.

**Genesis:** R[em]ember that time you were copyin[g] out the Book of Genesis to practice y[our] hand-writing?

**God:** With l[o]cations in Pennsylvania and central N[ew] Jersey. Adjust your antenna peop[le].

# Two Important Questions on Ant Individuality

Ever since the Ant volunteered
for the sleep and efficiency experiment
he's been tired.

The lab coats introduced him
to ennui. Now
he can't let go.

He's a dullard, he's aware of that.
In his animal trance
he is no prize, no finding

no culmination of tidy field-notes.
At least he has no memory
of first love.

*One ant asks the other:*
*Are you happy?*
*Why can't you sleep?*

# I'll come see you

> (response to Blok's "Angst")

You, in my heart, introduced me to your bird
of fear and you became my own
feathery voice of God.

Don't mistake me though for your other
bird, your hallucinatory and detailed excuse
for not returning my mundane calls.

I've hid you in plain sight along with many vices.
In this season of late nights I lost hope
in our bright-eyed cityscape.

Overheard: *Being young
is like being in a dream.*
But whose, I want to know.

To understand me you have to read this
which you can't (details later).

I dreamed we were cohabitating in an airy room
like a church outside, complete with battered wood
and no doors.

Stories, in fact, do circulate
about how people die
that turn out not to be true
like with Harry Houdini.

Always late.
In bed, reading Asimov

you get up for beer,
not getting up, then
really, not getting up.

Today, with this new information,
I don't remember any more, any less.
In these pictures I have here you don't age
or even blink.

I've faced it.
There never was an old or new man
rising in your heart-if-you-had-one.

# Letter to Legal Advice Columnist

Dear Rufus,

Last week in a parking lot at about 7 a.m.
I got this injury to my right foot.

The hotel called the police and I told them it was an accident.
But really it was more like someone (I know) slamming

the right front passenger car door on my foot.
I believe this could be called a road rage situation.

My kids got me to the E.R. later. I didn't want to go at first.
The E.R. people called it a crush injury

and said how this does not happen without the use of force.
Due to some things in my past I didn't want drugs.

I can tolerate a lot of pain but I was still begging
for drugs because I needed something

to make me forget
later what the pain felt like.

Rufus, I have had a fractured carpel tunnel and that pain
was not anything like this was.

I told the doctors and nurses about my anxiety,
diabetes, and attention deficit disorder medications.

My kids are telling me I should call the police
and change my story about the crush injury being
   accidental.

They say I was in some kind of shock, previously
and I should speak to a lawyer.

They say we could get a hold of the surveillance tape from
   the casino,
they have infrared cameras all over the place.

Maybe I should not have been there at all
but the tape will at least show what really happened.

That's why I am writing you for advice.
One weird thing is how in the E.R.

they found a staple in my foot and I don't remember
   getting that.
The doctor wants me to follow up on this, medically.

This person (that I know) has caused me a lot of mental
suffering and physical agony.

Should I sue?
Sincerely,

Mandy in Washington (State)

# A Point on a Map

Pull yourself together, sky.  Listen up!

It's not like you've been buried alive.

Everything is new to a new baby.

Red mourning happens in Acts 1 and 2.


More and more tree curtains and grasses bar entry. The tundra smells of new cars.

Try to tell the truth, for once.

Keep your eyes glued to the road.

They say, you can't watch the same movie twice.


Yesterday clouds spread across the ceilings of a series of movie sets.

The impulse is still there: Leave this country. Everything is not your fault.

That old shadow shows up like a new song cycle or the history of tango.

There are green, gem-like islands dotting our wide river.

No one gets a paycheck. A sixth sense: I'll never see him again.

# Here is my story, magic not included

You see this outline of a person, crouching behind glass, like behind a storefront. It used to be a place selling shirts and ties and such. Now it has handmade baby gown, Depression glass cake plate, silver cigarette case. Her paws want to grab that cake plate and hold onto it.

This storefront is the center of something. It's not an alcove. The storefront connects to money and food. Let's say this is about me since it is. The items in the storefront are clues hiding in plain sight, all about me. I thought this was a minor incident and that I'd have trouble remembering it.

Back then there was a picture in the living room of a ship in a stormy sea. That's how I got the idea I was a sea-vessel. I had some musical phrases in my head about that picture. One was like a quote from Marie Antoinette. I was all dissipated.

In the middle of this story I have to back up in my own footprints.

A friend of mine who hated me half the time made up this game. I would be blindfolded and pluck plastic eggs from her basket, known as the Basket of Fortune. The one I usually plucked was purple and turns you into a monkey, no, it just makes you think you are a monkey.

I didn't like talking on the telephone but was nevertheless always waiting for a call—The Call.

I had this car when I was nineteen that was maroon but everyone called it brown. It came with a postcard attached to the rearview mirror featuring the famous wide-eyed stare of Franz Kafka. Every time I looked in that mirror I saw his haunted and cloudy face. I probably should have discarded that face, but, I had a pretty fair idea that to do this would be wrong. Wrong so you shouldn't do it like how you aren't supposed to clip the tag off a mattress or kill a praying mantis.

Poverty may be relative. So may affection. Religion plays an important part in my life. At age ten, it made me keep wanting to look back. Luckily I never turned into salt. I just kept falling over my feet. That's what head over heels means. But all I really wanted was a live bird.

I kept wanting this specific, live bird I never got. I eventually did get a sense of renewal when I decided to let the musical phrases out of my head. I put them on pieces of paper and glued them all over telephone poles, mailboxes, corner fences, public restroom walls.

Are these the same streets, crossing left and right? I don't go back there much, I can't tell. If I get some money I will try more often. I will. I am a wrecked ship.

## B (KINDS OF DRAMMING)

~~[struck through]~~

It looks like a banana but really ~~[struck through]~~

(yours) Try to wake up ~~[struck]~~ Watch your back.

Delete prison time from your resume.

~~[struck through]~~

Black Box and Casing: Throwaway cameras are like those antique jokes littering Someone's verbal language fantasies.

Blanket: Seeing a weak loved one is twice as hard as seeing them strong.

Blow-gun: Killing someone in a church or while they sleep with a blow-gun is punishable ~~by death~~.

~~[struck through]~~ fish teeth and feathered to be somebody's fault.

# Two Important Questions Concerning Seahorses

*If we were seahorses and the men were impregnated
what would you take advantage of first?*

*And what would you be afraid of?
?????*

I would take the grand tour
and visit many large bodies of water

those I could reach in as many days,
and keep a diary.

I'd want to visit the Black Sea
and Lake Michigan, just to name a few.

I'd take advantage of all the latest
transportation thingies.

There must be some companies catering
to this kind of travel.  I'd keep in touch

with Papa Seahorse, a good guy
I wouldn't have to worry about while on tour.

He would basically refrain from consuming
alcohol and free-fall amusement park rides.

If I were a seahorse, I'd be really into motherhood,
what the hell,  and meeting my own assorted needs

higher and lower, and sometimes the needs of others.
I might forget about my family

while in the Black Sea,
or somewhere like that.

That old fear of forgetfulness might linger
in my seahorse consciousness.

# Fairmount Ave.

I saw a crow land on what seemed like the speckled roof of our country, but it turned out to be the deck of a small, rickety boat. I was smudged all over with white. The crow wore a hat made out of old, black and white newspaper. He was holding a finger in his beak. I can't swim and was distressed about being on or near a boat of any kind.

The crow's eyes swam with the wind.

I tried hard to have a happy thought, one I could remember and look back on later.

It was on that day that I lost my sense of smell. Aromatherapy and aroma attacks will have little if any effect on me now.

At the same time, assuming this happened when I was seven or eight, a fourteen-year-old girl was leaving her hungry and rumorous house-not-a-home, and for the last time. Our paths, the girl's and mine, crossed and re-crossed over the years, like the cuts skates make on the ice.

The fingernail on the finger in the crow's beak had a blue dot on it, like the blue dots I used to see on my father's nails as I watched him paint a wall or hammer a shingle. My father is always late to arrive, even in death.

The crow has something to say.  Let him speak.

# Incorruptible

The sun set. We saw it off. At that moment there was still an outside chance of being corrupted.

This waiter has flair. He has my cousin's nose. He takes the least number of steps. The dog looks on. I have a memory of my father lifting and carrying boxes of bread.

Just at that moment you spoke to the dog. You explained that we could not take him inside the building, so he'd have to loiter outside a bit longer. He was left to think about not belonging.

Why worry? Why count the broken hours? You say something like that to no one in particular, or to someone you love.

You assign the roles. I get to be the bad luck owl. Everything is steady, or tries to be, like we're on a stately barge. Everyone is alive again. Except for me. My paint is flaking away. Apples are falling pretty far from our trees. On nearby Hanover Street a once inviting and cared-for house has been recently demolished. An upright piano stands slightly elevated at the top of the front steps. Someone should remove it, but it looks nice there, surrounded by blue skies and summertime.

Just at that moment I was incorruptible. We were interrupted by the radio. You floated the idea and cloud-like, I rained.

# Acknowledgments

Much appreciation to the editors of the following publications for featuring these poems, sometimes in earlier forms. Also, special thanks to Daniel Dragomirescu and his team for sharing some of these poems with a Romanian audience. Heartfelt thanks to Carla Spataro, Christine Weiser, Courtney Bambrick and the PS Books crowd. Thank you to Jacklynn Niemiec for artistic inspiration.

"Two Important Questions Concerning Seahorses" (*Apiary*)
"Her dress shows she has abstained" (*Cheat River Review*)
"Here is my story, no magic included" (*Curatethis*)
"Incorruptible" (*Hanging Loose*)
"In the fire alley a rift opened up" (*Mead*)
"A Point on a Map" (*Philadelphia Stories*)
"I'll come see you" and "Fairmount Ave." (*Ping Pong*)
"Insomnia," "If You Dream About," "A Watch in a Dream," and "Kinds of Dramming" (SOUND:POETREE:: Fanzine)

Four poems here ("I'll come see you," "In the fire alley, a rift opened up," "Two Important Questions Concerning Seahorses," and "Incorruptible") also appear in *Reading Apollinaire*, a book with translations into the Romanian, part of the *Contemporary Literary Horizon* journal series.

www.ingramcontent.com/pod-product-compliance
Lightning Source LLC
Chambersburg PA
CBHW070049070426
42449CB00012BA/3198